POEMS OF EAST

Melbourne

Le-Hoa Wysham

To order additional copies of this book, contact:
Xlibris
AU TFN: 1 800 844 927 (Toll Free inside Australia)
AU Local: 0283 108 187 (+61 2 8310 8187 from outside Australia)
www.xlibris.com.au
Orders@Xlibris.com.au

ISBN: Softcover   978-1-6641-0180-7
         Hardcover   978-1-6641-0182-1
         EBook   978-1-6641-0181-4

Library of Congress Control Number: 2020921291

Print information available on the last page

Rev. date: 11/24/2020

Contents

Foreword

As a long- time resident of East Melbourne, I am passionate about the suburb's gorgeous historical buildings, its exquisite gardens and its rich Melbourne heritage and history.

I want to share my feelings and sentiments for East Melbourne, telling the story inscribed through my poems about special places, icons and famous identities that shaped the suburb, which go unnoticeable.

With much love and sincere thanks to my fairy and best friend Mary Cawse for her cornerstone support to my poems book project

Hot Air Balloons in Autumn Over Yarra Park

In blissful morning I stroll the cherished Melbourne Yarra Park

Morning dew, damp lush green lawns, and the still autumn air

Birds chirping, bike riders on paths covered in autumn leaves

Amusing happy dogs chasing their owners gathering sticks

Heart-warming, so uplifting, I ponder...how good life is.

Yesterday, the MCG stadium filled with excited and hyperactive fans

The mighty roar "Up there Cazaly" from thousands of fanatic footy clans

Melburnian's passions in footy seasons can't be denied

You love it, you hate it, but you can never knock diehard footy might!

I hear a ghastly sound and look up to the sky

Colourful balloons gently floating come into sight

White clouds, bright yellow and red balloons framing the heaven above

Giant airships with flashing flames, the air overwhelmed

What a breathtaking, bewitching and monstrous sight !!!

Spectacular hot air balloons in the Yarra Park autumn ...forevermore in my mind.

Treasury Gardens

Summer sun stretching its warm canopy over Treasury Gardens

Imposing high rise buildings watch the petite precinct park

Handsome Moreton Bay fig trees line the long extending footpath

A walking boulevard that seems endless with nowhere to land

Rock pool gardens lovingly circle the paved water pond

Water fountains sound pleasant and want to belong

Little birds chirp in tune, eliciting touching responses

Humming together a soothing melody all day long

Large solid rock standing erect with dignity for the JFK Memorial

People come from every corner of the globe to visit the world hero

He gave his life for his country, but sadly he had to go

I remembered as a child the day the assassin took JFK's life

The world stopped in shock and horror and people silently cried

He was one of a few good men, who forever will stand mighty

His love for the people, for life and his love for mankind

Rest In Peace JFK you left your stamp on world history

Deep in thought I whisper...... JFK be happy and free

Treasury Gardens a blissful place for many to reflect

Someone taking snapshots, happy photos of a nearby wedding

Rock gardens arranged strategically, enclosing the manmade oval pond,

Water fountain running calmly in rhythm to the lively bird song

Treasury Gardens just a few steps away from the gold storage Treasury Building

History of Golden Melbourne, once a rich city proudly displaying the bounty of gold mining

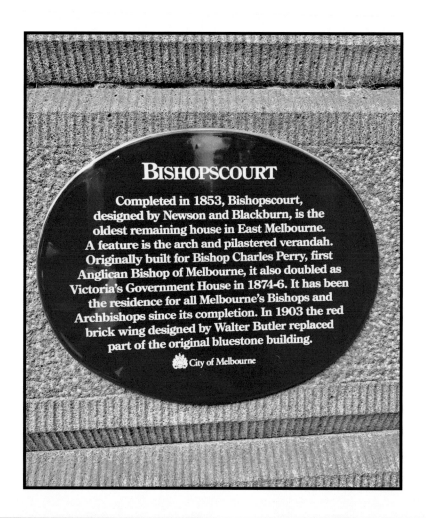

BISHOPSCOURT

Completed in 1853, Bishopscourt,
designed by Newson and Blackburn, is the
oldest remaining house in East Melbourne.
A feature is the arch and pilastered verandah.
Originally built for Bishop Charles Perry, first
Anglican Bishop of Melbourne, it also doubled as
Victoria's Government House in 1874-6. It has been
the residence for all Melbourne's Bishops and
Archbishops since its completion. In 1903 the red
brick wing designed by Walter Butler replaced
part of the original bluestone building.

City of Melbourne

Bishop Court

Founded in 1848, Bishops Court is one of the first houses built on Clarendon Street, East Melbourne

Designed by Newson & Blackburn, using blue stone construction in a style of gothic architecture

This landmark domain is listed on Victorian Heritage Register and the National Trust of Victoria

Assigned the official residence and office of the Anglican Archbishop of Melbourne

For 2 years, from 1874 to 1876 it's was the Victoria's Government House

Gracious Bishops Court has a very special place in Melbourne's garden history

James Blackburn's original design of an Italianate villa mansion is very picturesque

Representative of many famous Melbourne public buildings and boom-time homes

Inspired by the arts and crafts movement, customary for modern additions to classical buildings

In 1903, the turn-of-the century extension, the lavish red brick wing was added

The largest intact urban estate in the City of Melbourne, one of only seventeen buildings surviving

Sweeping lawns and fruits and vegetables all interwoven with a series of serpentine paths

The garden was designed in the Gardenesque style and features extensive tree plantings

Bishops Court survives today as one of Melbourne's oldest, finest iconic buildings

While the Archbishops, a metaphor for the Anglican Church, maintain position with dignity and visibility

The archbishops' wives made a significant contribution to Melbourne's religious, social and philanthropic life

Whose lives reflected the changing roles of women in the family, the church and society

Essentially a private home, in the past 160 years, Bishops Court has governed all the residents' lives

Hosting many memorable outdoor charitable Christmas parties held on the Bishop Court lawn,

Live music, children's games, fun raffles, food and wine and mingling with the local community

Bishops Court is an eminent part of East Melbourne's history, supporting women's revolutions in society

Sophie Lane – Charles La Trobe Poem

Sophie de Montmollin, of privileged birth, born in Neuchâtel, a small town in Switzerland near the French border.

It was here, she met Charles Joseph La Trobe, who came as tutor to her cousin Albert de Pourtalès.

They married in 1835 and spent their honeymoon at Jolimont, the family manor owned by the Pourtalès.

La Trobe was appointed Superintendent of Melbourne Port Phillip District, where the family settled in.

In 1839, Melbourne was an English colony and only four years young, a little shanty town

The La Trobe's erected their prefabricated cottage, named it Jolimont, just east of the town

The house no longer on its original site, exhibiting a slightly skewed front onto Sophie Lane

La Trobe's modest £800 salary and Jolimont, in spite of later extension, was only a small house.

Sophie was devoted to their four children and not the leader of society as the locals may have wanted

In 1850, Princes Bridge opened, Sophie's friend Georgiana McCrae stood in for her, no-one sought her out

She involved herself in charitable works, accompanying other society ladies often visiting female prisons

Here they taught needlework, a skill in demand, to prepare the women for life outside the institution

Sophie and her children returned to Switzerland in 1852 for the children's education to be prepared

Charles La Trobe resigned, waiting for eighteen months for his successor, Governor Hotham to be appointed.

Just a week before he sailed, he learned of his beloved Sophie's death in Switzerland three months earlier

A love story of the La Trobe's at the time during the early settlement, where Melbourne's history emerged

GOVERNOR LATROBE.

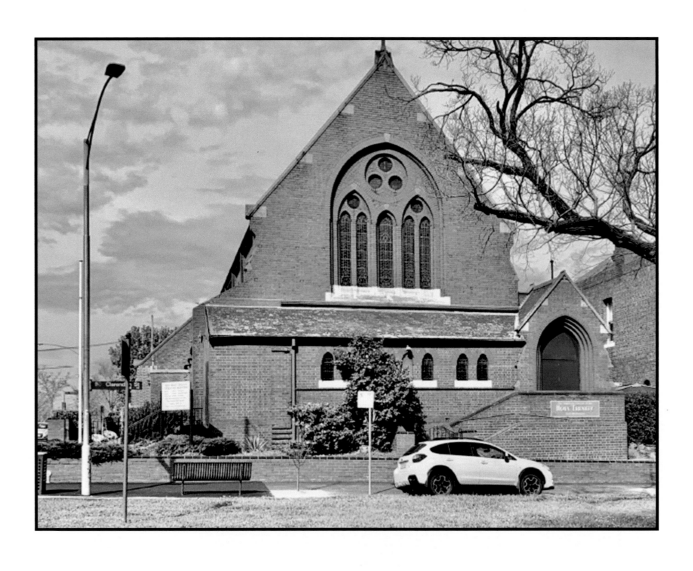

Trinity Place

Trinity Place runs between George and Hotham Streets and forms part of the original land grant to the Anglican Archdiocese

The grant assigned two acres of land to the Anglican Church and came to be known as the Cathedral Reserve

Bounded by Hotham, Clarendon, and George Streets, the parcel of land where the future Anglican Cathedral was to be established

The Church built a schoolhouse on the corner of Hoddle Street and Victoria Parade, it was the start of Holy Trinity Parish services

Early church services were held, serving the working-class families on the low-lying

Richmond and Collingwood commission blocks

Family mingling in circle, children standing beside their mothers; vivacious ladies in their lovely frocks

The congregation longing to build a parish church at the highly desirable Cathedral Reserve, an ideal and logical site

Initially the bishop refused to allow a parish church to be built, it had to be the chapter house to the new cathedral on the site

The new cathedral was built in Swanston Street, the parish church formalised its request, and the bishop's permission was granted

The new parish church was built in George Street, just east of Trinity Lane, the allotted Cathedral Reserve at the opposite end

New Year's Day, 1905, a horrendous fire destroyed the church, bluestone walls - a single pillar and one door left standing in grey ashes

The new church was rebuilt in 1906, the pillar and the door were incorporated into the design, today these all can be seen,

The Holy Trinity Church stands proudly elevated on the present corner site, providing wonderful daily services for the loyal masses

Wedding, baptisms and friendly traditional services, the church is committed to make the love of Christ known, and to serve the community in His name

The Tale of Two Cathedrals

The St Patrick's Cathedrals in Melbourne and New York City are the two largest cathedrals in the globe

In 1858 the building commenced on both decorated Gothic churches for the devoted to conventicle

The Cathedral spires are similar in height and both with the Neo Gothic Revival design

Both Cathedrals in New York City and Melbourne City are designated national historic sites

I have been to many places, visited many Cathedrals in a myriad of major cities on my wander

I have fond recollections of both St Patrick's Churches, as I have lived in both cities and still remembered

Watching white snowflakes dancing over St Patrick's, in the blistering cold of a New York winter,

And leisurely strolls in Fitzroy Gardens, breathe in the fresh cut hay in warm Melbourne summer breeze

The crystal chiming of St Patrick's Cathedral bells is heart-warming, sets me pondering about all the places I have been.

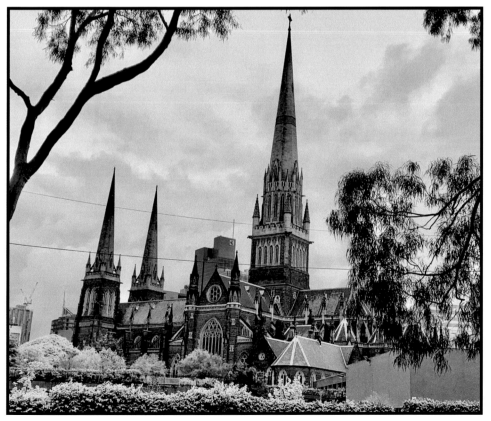

Old Treasury Building

The Treasury Building is considered one of Australia's finest Renaissance Revival buildings

Built from wealth accumulated during the Victorian Gold Rush, and constructed in Palazzo form

The building was proposed to house some of that wealth in the 'gold vaults' in the basement

Museum of Melbourne, hosts the original gold vaults where gold bullion was stored during the gold rush era

By the time it finished the gold rush was over, and hence it was used to store government documents

Young architect J. J. Clark,, who was just 19 years of age, designed the building which gave him fame

Throughout the building, rare historic documents in the museum and many of J. J. Clark's drafts are on display

It's the "finest public building exterior in Australia", architectural historian Miles Lewis once described

As a leading public building in Melbourne, located in a prominent position with open space around it

Notable as the financial foundation of the city it creates an important perspective at the Collins Street top end

The Old Treasury comes to life with many celebrations including the AFL Grand final parade and major public events

Darling Square – a Little Oasis

From the Simpson Street tram stop, a gentle stroll to Darling Square...

Darling Square, a peaceful oasis in the secluded Darling Street

Single cottages assemble on Grey Street, graciously overlooking this pretty square

Contrasting with the charming Victorian manors standing grand on Gipps Street

I bask in Darling Square, breathe in the fresh grass in warm summer air

Watching the hasty walker, chatting while tossing back her cherry-red hair

Riders in the horse carriage, loping pleasantly along Simpson street

Song birds singing, whistling a happy tune, sounds cheerily sweet

The big century-old oak tree extending its wrinkled arms

Like a mother standing still, waiting, reaching for her beloved child

An attractive couple settled in green folding chairs, sipping sweet summer wine

A breathless young woman chasing her toddler tirelessly in the dappled sunlight

Mosspennoch House

Hayes Lane

The stories of how the lanes are named, encapsulate the rich diversity of East Melbourne's heritage

In the 70s, public concern regarding "land scandals "led to a Royal Commission

Former Housing Commission officers were convicted of fraud, conspiracy and bribery

Geoffrey Hayes and Brian Dixon, failed to exercise control over the department's illegal conduct

Spent vast amounts of government funds, purchasing unsuitable land at hideously high prices

Speculators and land developers, pocketing their "got and gain" with cheerful delight

Despite failings as Minister of Housing, Geoffrey Hayes left behind a great legacy to East Melbourne

He supported conservation of the historic fabric of the suburb over development

And instrumental in saving from demolition Clarendon Terrace at 210 Clarendon Street,

Crathre House, on the corner of Powlett and Gipps Streets, still occupying its ground

Braemar, in George Street were preserved intact as a result of Geoffrey Hayes' negotiations.

East Melbourne's lanes are recognised as an integral part of its historic character and evolution.

Hayes Lane, named after Geoffrey Hayes, the disgraced Minister of Housing, under the Hamer government

Cairns Memorial Church

English Gothic Cairns Memorial Church, formerly Presbyterian, with its impressive architecture

History recalled, in 1988 a disastrous fire, it is only the church's outer walls that survived

The burnt gutted church was left with only the sand stone facade standing to remember it by Eleven award-winning apartments were designed in 1995, to save the angelic historic holy site

131 Powlett Street now residential apartments; a heaven on earth with stunning external majestic appearance

Years old stained-glass church windows, rich hardwood flooring, stunning black glass roof up high

Magnificent apartments radiate luxury and some with a wrap-around beautiful terrace

Breathtaking views of marvellous Melbourne CBD and the Dandenong Ranges are in sight 130 years ago, a devoted congregation sat in rows singing glorious hymns, praying with faith

The handsome and elaborately decorated organ playing supreme sweet holiness tunes

The mighty Gods we worship in our life may be different, but really are the same Gods; so let it be

This holy ground affirming love for its residents living as happily and blessed as they can be

A brilliant transformation of modern residence in harmony with a heritage church

It is unique, divine, angelic it beguiles and delights the eyes of the beholders with much glee

In my daily walk, I often admired this ingenious, striking architecture splendour

A trip to visiting East Melbourne, the Memorial Church converted to apartments are a must to see

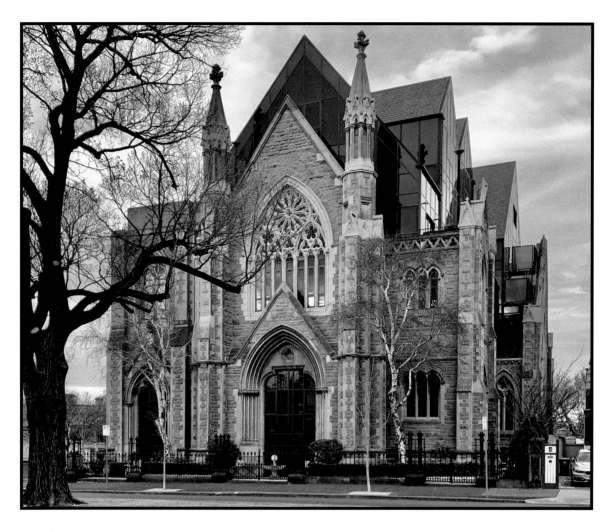

Albert Lane – Victoria & Albert love story

Albert lane runs off Albert Street, East Melbourne on the north side, just east of Powlett Street.

Named after Prince Albert of Saxe Coburg Gotha, Queen Victoria's beloved husband

There are eighty-two separate thoroughfares named after Prince Albert in Melbourne Streets

Queen Victoria was 'utterly devoted to him, he was more important to her than anything else in the world'

Prince Albert was entrusted with the running of the royal household and modernized the royal finances

He was an energetic man, a lover of the arts and of science; as a prince consort, initially he felt constrained

His reputation for supporting public causes and responsible for education reforms in university education

To celebrate industrial age achievements of 1851, Prince Albert was heavily involved in The Great Exhibition

The exhibition, a fund raiser, was an outstanding success, after being greeted at first with some suspicion

This money was used to found Victoria and Albert Museum, a world leader of art and design in South Kensington

He became the Chancellor of Cambridge University and President of the Society for the Extinction of Slavery

Victoria and Albert a remarkable royal love story, in the time of history of the great British Empire expansion

Their marriage bore nine children, who all followed tradition and married into the royal houses of Europe

Cook's Cottage

The Great Ayton family cottage is the only concrete historical link we have with Captain Cook's origins

James Cook, the famous navigator, almost certainly visited his parents, but did he ever live in the house?

Cook's Cottage built in 1755, originally stood on an extremity of the village of Great Ayton, Yorkshire

In 1933, the last owner of the cottage, Mrs. Dixon decided to put the cottage up for sale to the highest price

Prominent industrialist and philanthropist Melburnian, Sir Russell Grimwade bought the cottage for 800 pounds

Despite a difficulty, the patriotic Mrs. Dixon had stipulated that the cottage should remain in Great Britain

She was persuaded to accede to Victoria's claim as Australia was, after all, still "in the British Empire"

For this reason, she had rejected other offers of 300 pounds, supposedly from "wealthy Americans"

Dismantled and shipped to Melbourne in 253 packing cases, arriving April, 1934 to be reconstructed

A succession of owners following the Cook family's occupation, had altered the cottage structure considerably

Australian assemblers had the task of restoring the cottage accurately, to its mid-18th century appearance

A site in the Fitzroy Gardens was selected to complement the cottage with its large shady European trees

When the house was re-erected, cuttings from ivy adorned the house taken and planted for authenticity

Furnish it with centuries-old antiques, and blend in with a garden characteristic of the eighteenth century

The cottage was handed over to the Lord Mayor, H. Gengoult Smith, by Grimwade during a centenary ceremony

As a gift to present to the Victorian people on the anniversary of the settlement of the City of Melbourne

The cottage has undergone two restorations, the first was undertaken in the late 1950's and recent in 1978

Today it's the oldest house in Australia, a popular tourist attraction for visitors coming to Melbourne

As a volunteer Guide for the City of Melbourne, I was fortunate to worked at this grandiose historical site

I have had tremendous pleasure to tell the story of Cook's Cottage to the visitors; nurturing history alive

Winter Rain in Fitzroy Gardens

I looked up and saw a big dark grey sky

Mass clouds gathering at a great height, the rain bucketing down

Shadowing and shuttering, our marvellous Melbourne town

Rain, pouring rain, shivering and refreshing winter rain.....

City skylines impose amongst the old Moreton Bay fig.

While the oldest home, Cook's cottage, for two centuries remains

Elms lining the paths resemble tall soldiers standing guard

Yellow daffodils, white jonquils, perfume, profusion the flowers terrain

I walked briskly past River God Fountain in the chilled winter breeze.

All of a sudden St Patrick's Cathedral bells ring; my hearts beats

Fitzroy Gardens ravishing splendid following the rain

How fortunate we are to inherit this gorgeous domain

Scarred Tree

I spend many days walking in the Fitzroy Gardens admiring the scarred tree.

Pondering the way, the Aboriginal people removed bark from trees to make things like canoes

They used the wood and bark to build temporary shelters and large containers, spears and shields

Toe holes were cut for ease of climbing, and trees used as the lookouts in the hunt for bush foods

The Kulin group was the first people in Melbourne and Port Philip Bay to guard the land

The five language groups connected through shared moieties are joining hands

They were the hunter gatherers and made a sustainable living out of our rich nation's land

Waa (crow) is the protector of the waterways for the fishing of the rich food sources

Bunjil (wedge-tailed eagle) is the creation spirit of the Kulin nation and leads the way

The scarred tree is an important link to Aboriginal culture and a past spiritual life

A reflection on how the indigenous people took care of the land with resilience and innovation foresight

They extend up the Goulburn River Valley and into the Great Dividing Range

I pay respect to our Indigenous peoples who are the traditional owners and guardian of this land

Mary Mackillop Heritage Centre

Mary Mackillop Australia's remarkable first Saint of the Catholic Church

Founder of the Sisters of St Joseph of the Sacred Heart, well known to thousands of Australians

A shy but determined young girl with a strong sense of religious vocation

Courageous, committed individual who has won a permanent place in Catholic history for a woman

In her younger age, working and supporting her family and siblings

Her strong love for God, desire to do what she could for people in need

It was the Aboriginal children who gained most of her attention

She taught the local children in the church of her home for religious education

Mary Helen MacKillop (1842-1909), known in life as Mother Mary of the Cross

Fulfilment of her dream devoting her life to God, and desire to serve the poor

Mary's finest feature was her large blue eyes, affectionate but determined

Her charity towards her neighbour was outstanding, her virtues were multitudinous

Those who had joined her would need a Rule of Life

"Live poorly, own nothing in their own right

Depend on Divine Providence on their subsistence

Go where ever they needed, do all the good they could

Never see an evil, without trying to see the remedy"

Mary MacKillop Heritage Centre East Melbourne a place of inspiration and vitality

Manifests and promotes the spirit and charisma of Saint Mary

Visitors are welcome to the Centre to view the Temporary Art on display

Don't forget to take home a special gift from their exclusive gift shop and museum

The Fairies Tree in Fitzroy Gardens

A must ....to visit the famous Fairies Tree in the wonderful Melbourne Fitzroy Gardens

Immerse, listen to the winds whisper a fairy tale story over hundred years ago

The Fairy Queen was born to earth and with her magic transformed the gardens to live

Red Gum tree sprung its seed provided the Fairy Queen a tree home, they all come alive

Old Frog, Wise Magician, Old Owl, Eagle, Emu and Spider the Old Sorcerer

Stout heart riding his Bullfrog, Kangaroo, Wombat, Dingo and a Reading Mother

Narrate a story of the Fairy Queen and The Big Tree legend adventures together

Wonderstruck children visit the Fairies Tree and gather its enchanting history, the myth lives on

The notable sculptor and children's author, who carved The Fairies Tree, is Carola (Ola) Cohn

Her work was inspired by the Elfin Tree in the beautiful Kensington Gardens, London

Around the world, her art is displayed widely beside her collected prized sculptures

Her home in 43 Gipps Street, a school for learning arts and a Memorial Centre

The Fairies Tree, Ola Cohn's gift to Melbourne's Children endures as a heritage sculpture

Ola Cohn Place

Sculptor Ola Cohn acclaimed for her most loved work in the Fitzroy Gardens, the Fairies' Tree

Had a long association with East Melbourne; she bought the old livery stables at 41-43 Gipps Street

Ola (originally Carola) was born in Bendigo in 1892, her father was a brewer of Danish origin Ola only ever wanted to be a sculptor from the time when she was a small child modelling on the beach

Her first step was enrolling in art and sculpture classes at the Bendigo School of Mines

The same time attending life drawing classes at the Victorian Artists' Society in East Melbourne

She studies at the Royal College of Art in London, one of her lecturers was the famous Henry Moore

Her work in stone, wood, terracotta and bronze, are displayed in most state and provincial galleries

The timber cover of the font at Holy Trinity Church, East Melbourne is her mark to the community

The large stone figures of Science and Humanity at the Hobart General Hospital won her a major prize

Her home 41 - 43 Gipps Street became a popular art studio for women from all corners to come, learn and try

A great meeting place for artists and the permanent home of the Melbourne Society of

Women Painters and Sculptors

Menzies Lane – Sir Robert Menzies

Menzies Lane in recognition both of Sir Robert Gordon Menzies Australia's longest serving Prime Minister

And the Menzies Foundation which has its home in Clarendon Terrace, on the north side of the lane

Robert Gordon Menzies, a brilliant student, winning scholarships to his primary school, Grenville College

Continuing with scholarships to his secondary school, the prestigious Melbourne Wesley College

He studied Law at the University of Melbourne, graduating in 1916 with first class honours

Successfully admitted to the bar and a well-known KC by 1929 in Victorian Law courts

Four months before the beginning of World War ll, he first became Prime Minister, leading his party

The Curtin Labour party to take over the government due to Menzies party unfortunately split

Menzies founded the new Liberal Party, and was elected the inaugural leader of the party

He led the opposition as the head of a Liberal-Country Party which returned government in coalition

His appeal to home and family, reassuring via regular radio talks and public promotions

Matched the national mood as the economy grew and middle-class values prevailed

In memory of Sir Robert Gordon Menzies which the Menzies Foundation honours, today an effective operation

It was established through donations in 1979 and is a non-profit, non-political organization Established to promote excellence in health research, education and post-graduate scholarships by Australians

Menzies remain our great Prime Minister in total for 18 years, retiring at 71 years of age; who served the nation skilfully.

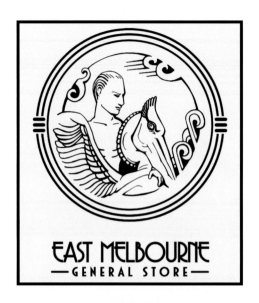

East Melbourne General Store

East Melbourne Emerson Dairy, owned by Mrs Emerson on beautiful Hotham Street

Fresh veggies and home-made produce was added to the expanded store in 1862

Original bluestone building transformed to the current dwelling, set in a quiet treelined street

For over 150 years, still selling 70's iced doughnuts and good old ice cream "cones"

Old man with his faithful dog by his side, sitting at the shop front terrace

Indulge in pastries, sipping fresh hot brewed coffee, enjoy bright early morning sun

Leisurely reading, rustling sounds of local newspaper, from back to front

Family entering with children laughing, holding back the little puppy as it wants to run

East Melbourne General Store continues with tradition of divine family treats

Hot pies, milkshakes, fresh veggies, wine, gifts, yummy home-made soups and sweets

Serving the local community with conventional "old school" style and kindness ever since

Fabulous to shop at the East Melbourne General Store, a place where people meet

Magnolias In Spring

I cherish walking in East Melbourne...the streetscapes timeless, unspoilt

Deciduous magnolia trees blooming on Powlett in spring

Pink creamy flowers like a child's soft silky skin

I halt and admire an abundance of tiny adorable flower buds

Peeking innocently through thick, waxy, glossy bushy green

Gorgeous magnolia blooms light up the gardens in the street

Large attractive flowers in full blossom, beaming and hypnotic

Magnolias aromatic fragrance is spellbinding and unforgettable........everlasting sweet

Wellington Gardens – A Georgian Village

In a quiet treelined street, Wellington Gardens is well tucked away from crowds

Georgian building village styles overlook the leafy greens

Immersed in peacefulness, sedateness and tranquillity is this enclave

While located on the edge of the CBD and various local parks

Serene courtyards and fountains trickle water, a heavenly cul-de-sac

The Lord Wellington Club a gathering place to get acquainted

Outdoor terraces, lofty ceilings, mezzanine apartments with Juliette balconies

Surrounded by gorgeous gardens, an irresistible and alluring place to be

Wellington Gardens is a sought-after location for a prized lifestyle

I have many fond recollections of happy time living there

Yarra Park State School

Originally built Circa 1874 this historic building sits proudly on the national trust register

Prize winning design for a government school by architect Charles Webb, the building has much to offer

Tudor style in polychrome brick with restrained ornamentation, in the Victorian period and Neo-Gothic

Quietly positioned, well-executed and restrained apartments transform the former Yarra Park School.

Grand in stature and impressive in scale, one can marvel at the lifestyle and sophistication apartments

Over 140 years ago, a place of history, where Yarra Park Primary School students once studied

The post-war housing shortage meant couples and their children were living with their parents.

"Miss Hammond, she was a lovely little lady and very, very strict that was how the teacher was,

I remember getting the 3ft ruler across the back of my legs for talking. " It was a way of disciplining.

"Ms. Sally McNabb as my Grade Prep teacher was wonderful" a former student recalled.

It was sad to see the school close and the children moved on, but at least the building was saved

Today the soaring ceilings remain, complemented by modern luxury and a divine timber stain

Highlighting its incredibly high ceilings and bright natural light, make a perfect inner-city domain

Incorporating a well-appointed kitchen featuring marble and stainless steel for the chef's satisfaction

Ideally positioned moments away from the Melbourne Cricket Ground, with Jolimont train station

Wellington Parade trams and Bridge Road shops and cafes are all within easy walking distance

Yarra Park State School in East Melbourne, its enduring history will be remembered for years to come

Hotel Windsor

Webb Lane – Charles Webb

Webb Lane runs alongside Yarra Park State school adjacent to the famous Melbourne Cricket Ground

Old period cottages and modern townhouses, blend together in the neighbourhood enclaves

Quaint bluestone cobbled lanes, horse trotting sounds on its path lead to the popular Yarra Park ground

Named after Charles Webb a resident of Brighton, renowned and brilliant Melbourne architect

Yarra Park State School, listed by the National Trust, one of his many government prizewinning projects

Royal Arcade, Windsor Hotel, Mosspennoch house, these are exquisite, elegant and timeless buildings

Webb's designs over centuries inspires and influences the circle of architectural innovation

Melbourne's golden era was blessed with his dedicated and ingenious architectural creations

Charles Webb, a founder of the Victorian Institute of Architects, a teacher, a mentor, a life of imagination

The Tale Of Two Parks

Famous New York Central Park in numerous people's "bucket list"

The Melbourne Fitzroy Gardens, a smaller scale with many parallels

Magnificent rectangular grounds in the centre of two dynamic cities

Sky scrapers tower over the parks watching the crisscrossing tree lined paths

A visit to Bethesda and River God Fountains so peaceful and glorious

At the outer, hawkers serving street food to happy passing by

Bikers, walkers, and joggers enjoy their physical rituals of enjoyment

Old fashioned horse carriages transporting travellers, admiring the city with delight

Trotting gently past the beautiful bride at a stunning wedding site

Lovely little Squirrels and shy Possums, exquisite, adorable intrinsic wildlife

St Patrick churches, two large distinguished iconic cathedrals of the world

Central Park and Fitzroy Gardens both are astonishing, forever abandon me for words

One Powlett

One Powlett, exceptional impressive building with quality and leisure in mind

Designed by acclaimed architect Nonda Kastalidis added to its name

Prominent position above the well-loved and desirable Laurent French Bakery

In addition to the local strip, abundant epicurean restaurants for the foodie

All the city's most loved attractions, just a hop-step from tram and Jolimont station

Fitzroy Gardens, bike tracks, leisure walks and Yarra River all accessible easily

Exceptional apartments with amazing sights of the vast city skyline in its entirety

Pop the champagne and immerse in the spectacle fireworks of lights in New Year's Eve

The entertainers with luxury apartments with huge outdoor living terraces

Complements in the distance, the panoramic uninterrupted vista of the Dandenong Ranges

Enjoy a relaxing weekend and have a merry time with beloved family and friends

Fanatic footy fans dream of apartments with magnificent MCG views lit up at night

Life at One Powlett, a finesse of sophistication which everyone envies

Powlett Mews

Powlett Mews runs west from Powlett Street, a dead-end lane, the rear access to 17 Powlett Street

The name 'Mews' attached to the lane sometime later, rather than in the original subdivision

Powlett Street was named after Frederick Armand Powlett (1811-1865) a public servant

Commissioner of Crown Lands for the Port Phillip District from 1840-1860. He had a mission

It was Powlett who, in 1855, granted permission to the young Melbourne City Council

To take control of the large area of Fitz Roy Square and the smaller adjacent land

Powlett placed firm conditions with the grant, including rules that should be strictly observed

"No roads for wheeled vehicles made through the gardens, and to be made into a people park"

A flowing stream running north-south between the two untouched swampy land areas

Originally a creek draining into the Yarra River, the land was largely used as a rubbish dump

The gardens are home to rainbow lorikeets, ducks, powerful owls, flying foxes and brushtails, ringtail possums

Clement Hodgkinson, who initially designed the gardens, with the planting by park gardener, James Sinclair

Landscaped with ferns and 130 willows, as a dense woodland with meandering English elm avenues

The creek smelling foul from the houses of East Melbourne's sewage continued to fill the air

After 50 years, the creek water was used for irrigation and substantially improved the site

Then mains sewerage was installed to the residences of East Melbourne with much delight

Our history recognised Commissioner Powlett's contribution

He also became the inaugural Melbourne Cricket Club President

Lorikeet

Powlett Reserve

Powlett reserve well equipped with social amenities for the local community

Bordered by rows of tall date palm trees and merging white paperbarks

Activities and family fun for all seasons, no need to look very hard

Child Care Centre definitely a happy place for playful little toddlers

The tennis club buzzing with players, full of interactive tennis games

Skate rider on the footpath skilfully makes a sudden swerve

Up in the air, the pigeons panic and squeal in turmoil

Little dog on a leash, grunting, whining and running in a circle

Its owner walking slowly, deep in thought, doesn't even notice

Youngsters swing on the monkey bars, laughing in the children's playground

Having fun and games with mum, dad chatting and stationed around

Picnic tables spreading with foods, preparing and assembling the family meals

A sense of community contentment at Powlett reserve fills the air … it's so endearing

Don the Masks

Beat the virus COVID-19; we must don the masks

Designer masks vs colourful footy masks

Plain simple masks vs bright funky cheerful masks

Hospital P2 masks vs disposable masks

Some use masks to highlight their smoky eyes

Scarves, bandanas, socks cleverly used as masks and get by

Three-layer masks, valve masks vs full face shield masks

Whatever you do you are not to leave home without a mask

Abominable, protesting, displeasing, we are trying our best

Bravo to resilience brave Melburnians standing to the test

Remember this is not forever, it's just right for now

Understandable, but I wish it would stop soon, somehow

Victoria Brewery – TriBeCa Building

Melbourne in the 1800s, a rich city built on the opulence of gold-digging trails

Gold miners after a hard day work, quenched their thirst with well-liked colonial ales

Old Victoria Brewery built in 1882, known as the home of beer, glorious beer

Striking façade designed by William Pitt, characterized the period of the years

Castellated façade, arched laneways, stamped and renowned...a local East Melbourne landmark

Early colonial brewer Thomas Aitken was regarded as socially influential

"Good beer, has been regarded as being among the necessities, rather than the luxury of everyday life"

Not everyone loved beer, temperance crusaders remonstrated to have alcohol banned

But with WWII Victoria Brewery's production of beer continued to expand

In the 60s, when locals complained about noise, finally the banning of the brewery

Forced to close, after 129 years of continuous operation, "beer - glorious beer"

Heritage-listed Victoria Brewery sold in 1985, marked the end of an era

The site reconstructed in 2004 into a lovely apartment building named TriBeCa

Retaining the historic façade, and the striking interiors designed by prominent Philippe Starck

Traditionally tall windows, lofty ceilings, elegant New York marble harmonizing with stainless steel

Heated outdoor pool, rooftop sun deck, gymnasium, IGA, cafes and trendy wine bar

Cohen Cellars, Old Brew Tower, Middle Brew Tower the only original buildings to remain

Australian Wild Life in Fitzroy Gardens

I adore the intrinsic wildlife playing "hide and seek" in the Fitzroy Gardens

I walk in the gardens at dusk to find the flying-foxes and my little possum friends

Cheeky little Brushtail Possum sitting on the tree branch, with bright eyes staring at me

The ringtail possum, hidden in his secret communal drey, nesting in the hollow of the tree

Nocturnal creatures love their solitude but are highly adapted to living near humans at night

Their friends are the grey-headed flying-foxes, the hard-working night shift, the "little Aussie battlers"

Flying out at dusk to feed on flowering nectar trees, delicious fruiting plants, acting like hustlers

On a summer's day, people sun bathing occupies the green lawn of this beautiful park

Sharing conversations, drinking and chatting while the children cheerfully laugh and play

A flock of Rainbow Lorikeets appears in the sky, flapping wings then disperse off in pairs

Aggressively defending their nesting and feeding territory, in the loudest noise of despairs

Sitting on the tree, their bright rainbow colours, gorgeously embossed in the bluest clear sky

A picture of multiple colours, blending in with nature, perfectly framing the tree top has caught my eye

A family of Wood Ducks, pecking for grasses and grains, slowly waddling across the ground

Mother duck making a loud "gnow" sound calling her ducklings, to come to socialise

A golden-haired child, watching the paddling ducks attentively, open-mouthed in her excitement

These delightful intrinsic animals are protected as part of the wonderful distinctive Australian wildlife

LADY FLORA HASTINGS.

Lady Hastings Lane

Lady Hastings was the occupier of 61 Grey Street which backs onto the lane

Lady Hastings Lane was named after her according to the 1889 rate books

Sadly, this is the beginning of the search and where the mystery remains

Over the years, no Lady Hastings has been documented as living in Melbourne

One real possibility for our Lady Hastings is the Hon. Elizabeth Harboard (1860-1957)

She believed to married George Manners Astley, the 20th Lord (Baron) Hastings

Lord Hastings was at the Melbourne Cup in 1888, that was covered in the famous social pages

Not a whisper about his wife, nor is there any reference to the couple at any stage.....

Serenity of Life

I saw a couple walking in the park

Hand in hand and marching, their steps apart

Immersed in themselves chatting and laughing in harmony

So wonderful to love and to be in love

I wondered, could it be me?

I saw a little girl playing in the park

The mother watching her child with a happy smile

I was once a child playing in the park

I watched the mother care for her child, I was there alone

I saw a bird flying away from the tree

Taking chances, North, South, East or West?

It does not matter little bird, fly away and be free.

As if it was me,

I am so glad to be free!

I saw a man singing in the rain

Jubilation while walking to catch the train

I saw an old man sitting on the garden bench

Lines on his faces, observing people come and people went

Life begins with the first breath we take and

Life ends with the last breath we have, but

Love has no beginning and love has no end

Dance like no one is ever watching

Love like you have never been in love

Live like there is no tomorrow

Serenity is what you can create and

Happiness is a state of your mind